Getting Old SUCKS

by
Ed Strnad

Illustrations by
Lidia Hasenauer

CCC PUBLICATIONS

Published by

CCC Publications
9725 Lurline Avenue
Chatsworth, CA 91311

Manufactured in the United States of America

Cover © 1997 CCC Publications

Interior illustrations © 1997 CCC Publications

Cover & interior illustrations by Lidia C. Hasenauer

Cover colorization by Dwight Wanhala

Cover/Interior production by Oasis Graphics

ISBN: 1-57644-048-6

If your local U.S. bookstore is out of stock, copies of this book may be obtained by mailing check or money order for $6.95 per book (plus $2.75 to cover postage and handling) to: CCC Publications, 9725 Lurline Avenue; Chatsworth, CA 91311.

Pre-publication Edition - 4/97
First Printing - 9/97
Second Printing - 9/98
Third Printing - 9/99

Acknowledgments

"Grow old along with me, the best is yet to be" —*Robert Browning*

Yeah, right.

This Baby Boomer Gone Bust wishes to thank others—who are also getting older bitchily—for their cranky contributions: Butch D'Ambrosio, Cliff Carle, JoAnn Strnad, Lidia Hasenauer, and my son Eddie, who keeps me from ever getting too old.

-E.S. kgnj65a@prodigy.com

Voting Republican
the first time

LIDIA

- Looking 40, acting 20, feeling 70, being 50

- Being older than the President of the U.S.

- Still needing to be another 30 years older before you can marry Anna Nicole Smith

- Still being 50 years away from having Willard Scott announce your birthday on TV

"If you're old enough to know better, you're too old to do it"

– George Burns

- Medicine bottle caps that suddenly turn into Rubik's Cubes

- Trading in your Porsche for a mobile home

- When you start thinking dark socks with sandals look attractive

- That you once hated injustice but now figure, why fight it?

- Bad days that make you wish you **had** run away with the circus

"By the time we've made it, we've had it"

– Malcolm Forbes

- That as your age goes up, everything else seems to come down

- Finally having to accept you won't ever hit a homer in game seven of the World Series

- Buying a red Corvette makes everyone think you're having a midlife crisis

- Being able to hide your own Easter eggs from yourself

- Not having to own antiques to have something really old to sit on

"The trouble with being old is there's so little future in it"

– Edna Frederikson

- Being unable to ride a roller coaster without fracturing something

- When you have all your teeth, but they're in a glass on the nightstand

- That without the first six cups of coffee in the morning, you're useless

- Childhood memories that fade, or become clearer

- Your back goes out more often than you and your spouse do

Gray hair on places that they don't sell dye for

LIDIA

- Driving a car large enough to land jet aircraft on

- Going from "hot" to "shot"

- Starting to resemble beef jerky wearing Nikes

- Learning to get along without one or two internal organs

"If I'd known I was gonna live this long, I'd have taken better care of myself"

– Eubie Blake

- Buying your first car with wood sidings

- Your kid's snickers when you put a compass on the dashboard

- Adolescent offspring who think you've transformed into a clueless moron

- The first time you're called a "Dirty Old Man"

- Becoming obsessed with that 3-letter word – *nap*

Hearing your favorite heavy-metal songs in elevators

- All new music sounds too damn loud, and you can't understand the lyrics

- Watching Paul McCartney morph into a jowly, grumpy geezer

- Cringing while watching Mick Jagger make a fool of himself on stage

- Another reunion of **The Monkeys**

"I'm not afraid of death,
I just don't want to
be there when it
happens"

– Woody Allen

- Getting an irresistible urge every winter to migrate to Florida

- When you finally have the answers to life, no one asks you any questions

- Being part of an intrinsically immature generation in its second childhood

- Endless arguments over Vietnam with people who weren't even alive then

- The jokes about not being able to see your belly button stop being funny

"Just remember, once you're over the hill, you begin to pick up speed"

– Charles Schultz

- Young people don't get your jokes any more

- Trimming head hair less often than nose hair

- Having to get up more than once a night to go to the bathroom

- The dreaded "Roto-Rooter" operation for male plumbing problems

- "Today may be the *last* day of the rest of your life"

"From birth to age 18, a girl needs good parents; from 18 to 35 she needs good looks; from 35 to 55 she needs a good personality; and from 55 on she needs cash"

– Sophie Tucker

- Being referred to as "a woman of a certain age"

- Wondering why it's called **men**opause when only women go through it

- Male menopause, also known as "the change of *wife*"

- Being unable to tell if you're having a hot flash, or an acid flash-back

- In order to look younger, you start hanging around with even older people

*"I have the rest of my life
to improve,
but it may take longer
than that"*

– Ashleigh Brilliant

- Bartenders who check your pulse instead of your ID

- People start saying "You look wonderful!" on your birthday

- Not walking when it says "Don't Walk"

- People who expect you to get "more spiritual" with age

- High blood pressure, high cholesterol, high anxiety, *low* sex-drive

"**When you are about 35 years old, something terrible always happens to music**"

– Steve Race

- Weird old rich people are "eccentric"; old poor people are just "crazy old coots"

- Cab drivers start calling you "Pops" instead of "Buddy"

- Sleep creases on your face that take 3 hours to go away

- Studying the obituary page for people who died younger than you

- Arranging single hairs in a snail-like pattern over your bald spot

When you get too old to flirt your way out of a speeding ticket

- Waking up one day to find shoulder-length ear hair

- When health food makes you sick

- When the only thing you exercise is caution

- After countless Kegel exercises you have the world's most well developed "kegel"

"I'm too young to be this old"

– Anonymous

- When your doctor warns you to slow down, instead of the police

- Turning off the lights for economic, not romantic, reasons

- Only hearing "Woo, woo!" when you're riding in an ambulance

- Buying a see-through nighty that your mate can't see through

- Being too young to take up golf but too old to run up to the net

"Those who welcome death have only tried it from the ears up"

– Wilson Mizner

- After turning 40, you seem to age at the rate of about 3 years per year

- After having kids, you age at the rate of 5 years per year

- Giving up New Age maxims for Old Age rants

- When you get aroused by that babe on **Murder, She Wrote** reruns

- Your personal license plate is "C NILE"

"Experience is the name everyone gives to their mistakes"

– Oscar Wilde

- Realizing that when your parents were your age, they were *ancient*

- Realizing that when Mozart was your age, he was dead 20 years

- Being unable to hold a phone number in your head long enough to dial it

- Wearing a "granny dress" makes you look like a real granny

- Hanging on to your bell bottoms, 8-tracks, and first spouse seems increasingly futile

*"I adore my bifocals,
my false teeth fit fine;
my hairpiece looks good,
but I sure miss my mind"*

– Anonymous

- "Evening wear" means a clean set of draw-string sweat pants

- "Getting lucky" means finding your car in the parking lot

- "Sexy Lingerie" means pajamas made of lightweight flannel

- "Safe sex" means not rolling out of the bed

- When a good-night peck on the cheek passes for your sex life 98% of the time

Watching your Pepsi-Generation turn into the Pepto-Bismol Generation

- Needing two brains (yours and your spouse's) to reconstruct one memory

- When 15 minutes seems like a long drive for a meal or a movie

- Being the oldest person at the rock concert

- Falling asleep 30 minutes into "Leno"

"Get it when you can, where you can, before you can't"

– Anonymous

- Gen-Xers who think the "Big Bopper" was a hamburger

- When birth-control becomes less important than birthday-control

- Your sexual preference changes – to younger people

- Sex, drugs, and Rock & Roll become chat rooms, melatonin, & Golden Oldies

- Being given a subscription to **USA Yesterday**

"Old age is when everything that doesn't hurt doesn't work"

– Anonymous

- Only feeling good when you see a photo of Keith Richards

- Your brain's memory is cluttered with annoying TV-show theme songs

- Needing to eat prunes on a daily basis

- When you go through an entire "2000 Flushes" in one week

- Falling asleep during sex instead of after it

"Anyone can get old. All you have to do is live long enough"

– Groucho Marx

- Suddenly wondering why the heck you're still shaving your armpits

- Resorting to slip-on shoes and only buying bras that fasten in front

- Searching madly for your glasses when they're perched atop your head

- Pucker-up marks around your mouth even when you're **not** sucking a lemon

- Failing eyesight prevents you from seeing how phony your toupee looks

"Death is the greatest kick of all, that's why it's saved for last"

– Anonymous

- You can't lift up or put down any heavy object without saying "HOO-BOY!"

- Giving up eating fatty food at the "Hard Artery Cafe"

- Giving up climbing up cliffs in favor of climbing into bed

- When your nicely rounded bottom becomes a widely flattened beam

- Beginning to look like your dog, especially if you own a **Shar Pei**

"Change is inevitable, except from a vending machine"

– Anonymous

- If you're male, your brain shrinks and your ears get bigger; if female, your spine shrinks and your boobs get longer

- Inexplicably becoming grouchier than a pit bull with a bowel constriction

- Regretting ever singing that rock song lyric, "Hope I die before I get old"

- Showing your age by remembering that Mary Martin played "Peter Pan" before Robin Williams did

- Calculating what your comic-book collection would be worth today had your mother not thrown them out

"The future ain't what it used to be"

– Anonymous

- Starting to glow softly in the dark after a lifetime of regular X-ray exams

- Pesky life insurance salesmen calling every day and night

- When your "gravy years" turn lumpy

- When your brain develops a phone-like "Memory Waiting" feature

- Looking in your bathroom mirror and thinking, "When did all this happen?"

Not doing drugs anymore because you can get the same effect just by standing up really fast

- Being stuck for an answer when your kids ask if you ever took drugs after they see the nude photo of you at Woodstock

- Your drugs of choice have become Zantac, Minoxidil, and Geritol

- Endlessly evaluating your life to see if it meant anything

- Getting creeped-out from seeing your name on a tombstone

*"Senescence begins
and middle age ends the
day your descendants
outnumber your friends"*

– Ogden Nash

- Looking older than Dick Clark

- Nasty germs you've always been immune to now jump up and bite you

- Not using a playground swing because of a fear of looking foolish

- How screwed up the younger generation seems as soon as you're no longer a member

- When a radio station calls your favorite songs "Dinosaur Rock"

"The man who views the world at 50 the same as he did at 20 has wasted 30 years of his life"

– Muhammad Ali

- The saying, "Only the good die young"

- Kids who use that old slogan "Don't trust anyone over 30" against you

- Finding "laugh lines" are nothing to laugh about

- Having obsolete skills, like knowing how to use a slide rule

- When your job title is preceded by "former" (e.g., former aerospace engineer)

"How old would you be if you didn't know how old you was?"

– Satchel Paige

- 50-somethings who are still living in the 60's

- 60-somethings still living in the 50's

- Aging Rock & Rollers who have overnight conversions to classical music

- Kids who think that goatees and tattoos are new

- Your major forms of exercise are: jogging your memories, exercising your judgment, and pushing your luck

*"Fun is like
life insurance;
the older you get,
the more it costs"*

— Elbert Hubbard

- Gaining weight and injuring bystanders with flying buttons

- Trying to keep your gut sucked-in on the beach

- Not being able to suck-in your double chin

- Cashiers who automatically give you the Senior Citizen's discount

- When you attempt to smooth-out the wrinkles in your socks, and realize you're not wearing any socks

"Death is Nature's way of saying, 'Your table is ready!' "

– Robin Williams

- "In-" and "Im-" words: incontinence; impotence; etc.

- Those obscene "F" words: forty, fifty

- That the Roman numerals for "40" and "Xtra Large" are the same (XL)

- When your age matches your pants size

- When a never-do-well kid moves back home

"A woman is as old as she looks before breakfast"

– Edgar Watson Howe

- Having a trick knee when you're not a magician

- Facial wrinkles give men "character," but give women only grief

- Outrageously over-priced skin lotions

- That vanishing cream doesn't really make you invisible

- Watching your youth go down the drain, along with your hair

When your knees start predicting the weather

- Fine print that keeps getting finer

- On the john, your legs start falling asleep quicker and quicker

- Eating dinner earlier and earlier

- "Sleeping in" means getting up at 6 a.m.

"The years between 50 and 70 are the hardest. You are always being asked to do things, and yet you are not decrepit enough to turn them down"

– T. S. Eliot

- Trying to reverse that vasectomy you got in your thirties

- Surprise-birthday parties after age 35

- People who subscribe to magazines like **Prevention**, as if death can be prevented

- Outliving everybody but the people you hate

- Saying "What did I come into this room for?" more than twice a day

*"Time is a great teacher,
but unfortunately
it kills all its pupils"*

– Hector Berlioz

- Becoming bugged by corruptions of the English language

- Firing off your first cranky Letter-to-the-Editor

- "Risk-taking" means eating a raw oyster, not flossing, telling off-color jokes at the office, and getting a tan

- When your belly enters the room a few seconds before the rest of you

- When your butt exits a room a minute after the rest of you

"Never trust a woman who tells her real age. A woman who would tell that, would tell anything"

– Oscar Wilde

- Not caring about going out Saturday nights anymore

- Your wife trusts you now

- Most of your mail is junk mail

- Most of your dreams are re-runs

- The News becomes your primary TV-fare

"Children are nature's very own form of birth control"

– Dave Barry

- You can still remember when **Saturday Night Live** was funny and William Shatner had real hair...

- But you can't remember who played the original Darrin on **Bewitched**

- That **Star Trek** is over 30

- That Johnny Carson isn't on anymore

- Being too grown up to collect **Star Wars** figurines

"Growing old is like being increasingly penalized for a crime you haven't committed"

– Anthony Powell

- Meeting an old flame after a 20-year interval, and wondering what the hell you ever saw in him or her

- Once-perfect figures racked by childbirth

- Realizing that the world will still spin merrily around after you die

- Becoming vociferously pro-death penalty

- That no matter how old you get, your parents will always treat you like a 6-year-old

"Age is a high price to pay for maturity"

– Tom Stoppard

- Starting to take wacky conspiracy theories seriously

- When alien abduction seems as good an excuse as any for your messed-up life

- Blowing 20 bucks a week on the lottery

- Seeing older women your age dating **much** younger men

- Realizing that life is a sexually transmitted disease that is 100% fatal

"Regrets are the natural property of gray hairs"

– Charles Dickens

- "Trophy wives"

- Playing videogame versions of bingo

- Playing the "Woulda-Coulda-Shoulda" game

- Needing industrial-strength shears to clip your toenails

- Being pulled over by a cop who's much younger than you

*"I wasted time,
and now doth time
waste me."*

*– Shakespeare
(Richard II)*

- Catching yourself frequently saying, "Is it just me, or is it HOT in here?"

- Catching yourself saying, "When I was your age..."

- Catching your foot tapping to a Lawrence Welk tune

- When your Help-Me-Up chair ejects you across the room

- Discovering that not only is life a bitch, it has puppies

When it takes assistance to blow out all the candles on your cake

- Saying "passed away" instead of "died"

- When you start wearing dorky glasses on a chain around your neck

- More than 6 candles on your **slice** of birthday cake

- Learning what your parents meant when they warned, "Just wait till you have kids of your own!"

"Men, like peaches
and pears, grow sweet
a little while before they
begin to decay"

– Oliver Wendell Holmes

- Trying to conceive a baby in your 40s

- When someone thinks you are your kid's **grandparent**

- Being a grandparent in your 40s and still trying to act cool

- Feeling like a failure because you never parented as well as June and Ward Cleaver

- When you finally become an expert at being a parent, the damn kid leaves home

"40 is the old age of youth; 50 is the youth of old age"

– Victor Hugo

- Envying people who are just 2 or 3 years younger than you

- Losing things: your glasses, keys, hair, memories, sense of humor, libido

- Closets full of stair-climbing machines, spandex, and Trivial Pursuit games

- Finding yourself discussing the weather for more than five minutes a day

- Using the word "angst" more than once a day

"Litigation takes the place of sex at middle age"

– Gore Vidal

- Seeing ancient-looking rock stars who were once your Teen Faves

- In the morning, hearing "Snap, crackle, pop" **before** you get to the breakfast table

- Boring others (and yourself) reminiscing about how they used to deliver milk, pump gasoline for you, etc.

- Derisive laughs from your kids when you tell them how you had to walk all the way across the room to change channels

- Previously hilarious exploding-cigar prank now causes a coronary event

"Q: How many 50-year-olds does it take to screw in a lightbulb?

A: None; their screwing days are long gone"

– A. Joke

- Emergency room visits for heart attack symptoms that turn out to be just heartburn

- No "past-ectomy" operations to cut off the effects of your reckless youth

- All the occupations you didn't become: astronaut, cowboy, fireman, ballerina, princess, actress, rock star, best-selling humor author, etc.

- Spending more time on the couch than your dog

- When your shrink says, "C'mon, you're old enough to know what to do"

Figuring out that in dog years, you're dead

LIDIA

- All this poetic crap about "surrendering gracefully the things of youth"

- When your spouse asks, "If I die, will you get married again?"

- After finally "getting all your sh*t together," you can't remember where you put it

- Being able to clearly see where you've been, but having no idea where you're going

"You know you're getting old when you've got money to burn, but the fire's gone out"

– Hy Gardner

- When your butt takes on the texture of large-curd cottage cheese

- When the butt-tattoo you got in your youth fails to amuse your proctologist

- Being unable to decipher tattoos on old wrinkled skin

- Having to drive around the parking lot for hours to get a spot close to the Health Club

- You're still in shape, but the shape is that of a sack of potatoes

"The last woman I was inside of was the Statue of Liberty"

– Woody Allen

- The only time you'll have a firm body again is when rigor mortis sets in

- That your body parts aren't covered by an extended warranty

- The fact that each day of your adult life 100,000 of your brain cells die and are never replaced

- The fact that the only things still growing are your ears and nose

- That Science will probably invent a Stop-Aging pill when you turn 80

"I must be getting absent-minded. Whenever I complain that things aren't what they used to be, I always forget to include myself."

– George Burns

- Eating healthy, exercising often, dying anyway

- Little pee-squirts when you laugh or sneeze

- Watching TV actors your age doing ads for adult diapers

- Getting to experience diaper rash again, but otherwise not feeling like a kid

- When you rationalize your naked self in the mirror by thinking "I was built for comfort, not for speed"

"A woman past 40 should make up her mind to be young, not her face"

– Billie Burke

- When your only sexual arousal comes from reading trashy Romance novels

- When spurts become dribbles

- Friends with lots of grandkids and wallets full of pictures

- Photo albums full of pictures of a younger, sexier you

- Seeing your wedding pictures after the divorce

"If my doctor told me I only have 6 minutes to live, I wouldn't brood, but I'd type a little faster"

– Isaac Asimov

- Pool parties with hard-bodied younger acquaintances

- Things that come with age, besides wisdom: wine snobbery, crabbiness, spouse dumping, and religious conversions

- Driving miles out of your way to save a few cents on a gallon of gas

- Calluses so far in-grown they reach another toe

- Cholesterol numbers higher than your SAT scores

Going from a two-piece bathing suit to a one-piece

LIDIA

- "Sweet 46" just doesn't have the same ring to it

- Giving up the beer, but keeping the belly

- Giving in and switching from jockey shorts to boxers

- Stiffness everywhere, except where you want it (and need it)

"I am sick of all this nonsense about beauty being only skin deep. That's deep enough. What do you want, an adorable pancreas?"

– Jean Kerr

- When the spirit is willing but the flesh isn't

- Eggs cooked "Over-50 Style" – half hard

- Reserving sex for special occasions, like the return of Halley's comet

- When your lover refers to your water bed as "the Dead Sea"

- Hearing the song "Born to Run" turned into a jingle for laxatives

"At 20 we don't care what the world thinks of us; at 30 we worry what it's thinking of us; at 40 we discover it isn't thinking about us at all"

– Anonymous

- Getting ribbed about taking an elevator up one floor

- When the only thing that you grow in your garden is tired

- Turning into Archie Bunker, or worse yet, Edith

- Forgetting important stuff, but being able to remember the combination to your high-school locker

- Remembering a time when you could buy whatever your heart desired with nickels and pennies

When your belt and shoes are both white.

LIDIA

- Looking like you feel

- Feeling like you look

- Starting to think you look spiffy with
  a hat or suspenders

- Starting to wear suspenders **and** a belt

"My dad's pants kept creeping up on him. By 65 he was just a pair of pants and a head"

– Jeff Altman

- When your pants creep up closer and closer to your armpits

- When **Nike** starts making orthopedic running shoes

- Being referred to as "absent minded"; "young at heart"; or "spry, for her age"

- Being disillusioned enough to know that horoscopes are crap, optimistic enough to still sneak a peek

- Lifetime membership in the Hair Club for Men

"If you get to 35 and your job still involves wearing a name tag, you've probably made a serious vocational error"

– Dennis Miller

- Seeing no evil (without glasses); hearing no evil (without hearing aids); speaking no evil (gossip's not evil, it's something to do)

- Coworkers who say, "It's about time" when you tell them you're thinking of getting a face lift

- Coworkers who ask, "When are you getting a face lift?" after you've gotten one

- Becoming so predictable, coworkers set their watches by your morning trip to the restroom

- On your list of "50 Things To Do Before I Die," only 2 things are crossed off

Having so many gall stones, they have to call in a geologist

- Being able to enjoy The Moment, but knowing it won't last

- Instead of having new milestones, you get new gall stones

- Blood pressure pills for the rest of your life

- When your Inner Child starts wearing mixed plaids and support hose

"All my life I've wanted to be somebody. But I see now I should have been more specific"

– Jane Wagner

- That awkward first day back to work after coloring your hair

- Coming home from work one day and discovering that your kids have all grown up

- Being unable to find a simple typewriter in an office full of computers

- You didn't make your first million by age 30, and 60 isn't looking good either

- Fearing that someday at work you'll be found slumped over your imitation-wood desk

"Happiness isn't something you experience; it's something you remember"

– Oscar Levant

- Younger people who make more money than you

- Waking up at 3 A.M., rethinking and regretting the dumb decisions you made in your 20s

- Being what some snot-nosed 8-year-old decided to grow up to be

- Worrying that someday your boss will discover you're just a big kid dressed in grown-up work clothes

- When your spouse's midlife fantasy involves moving to: the country/ Tahiti/Hollywood/a houseboat

"Middle Age is a time of life that man first notices in his wife"

– Richard Armour

- Starting to think your friends are acting really damn **old**

- Hearing your friends having spine-tingling discussions about retirement

- Getting tired of hearing, "You're not getting any younger you know"

- That lie, "You're not getting older, you're getting better"

- Watching a generation of aging hippies turning off, tuning out, dropping dead

"Never go to a doctor whose office plants have died"

– Erma Bombeck

- A vague but growing and nagging sense of **urgency**

- Getting a feeling that your days are numbered

- Going to McDonald's to read the newspaper

- Seeing someone in a store window and thinking "What a geezer" before realizing it's your reflection

- When grocery shopping, always having to buy food that's "good for you"

"Nothing is more responsible for the good old days than a bad memory"

– Robert Benchley

- Men who go into the woods to beat drums with a bonding group

- Having to eat yucky things, like parsnips, in order to set a good example for your kids

- Having to watch **Fantasia** with your kids and **not** get stoned

- When your upper arms flap in a stiff breeze

- That if your sinuses were as big as the Lincoln Tunnel, they'd still get stuffed

"A man is as old as the woman he feels"

– Groucho Marx

- Getting mammograms and knowing how lemons must feel

- Having your prostate examined by the **Incredible Hulk**

- When breasts go from "pert" to "pendulous"

- Fearing your gynecologist will find cave drawings on the walls of your uterus

- When you floss, and your bloody mouth looks like a losing boxer

"The secret of staying young is to live honestly, eat slowly, and lie about your age"

– Lucille Ball

- Your "spirit of adventure" means passing up the lobster bib

- When a phone in the bathroom becomes more important than mirrors on the bedroom ceiling

- Christmas becomes just a hassle

- Entertaining morbid thoughts that this Christmas might be your last

- When your spouse gives you appliances on your anniversary

Your hangouts change from the sports bar and the coffee house to the pharmacy and the bathroom.

- No compensation from the Tooth Fairy when your teeth fall out now

- Annual visits from the Bigger-Butt Fairy

- When your skin starts resembling the parchment of the Declaration of Independence

- When a hunk or a babe sidles up to you and asks, "Didn't you go to high school with my *mother*?"

"Old elephants limp off to the hills to die; old Americans go out to the highway and drive themselves to death in huge cars"

– Hunter S. Thompson

- Knowing that – contrary to what the Stones sang – time is **not** on your side

- You remember when Disneyland's "Tomorrow Land" looked futuristic

- Your day-planner book is basically blank

- Trying to look svelte with a size 40 waist

- When you can pinch an inch on your forehead

"The reason grandparents and grandchildren get along so well is that they have a common enemy"

– Sam Levenson

- Falling asleep in new situations, like at a stoplight

- Slow drivers annoy you, fast drivers scare you, and you're going from the latter to the former

- Your kids complain you drive too slow, and your parents complain you drive too fast

- Buying a car for the "ergonomics"

- Airbags can kill you

"If Shaw and Einstein couldn't beat death, what chance have I got? Practically none"

– Mel Brooks

- When your parents buy more gifts and toys for your kids than they ever bought for you

- When your childhood toys turn up in antique malls bearing astronomical price tags

- "Death of a Grandparent" is no longer a believable excuse for a few days off from work

- That the "peace" symbol now stands for Mercedes Benz

- Strobe lights now give you an epileptic seizure

"Go to bed; what you're staying up for isn't worth it"

– Andy Rooney

- When those 25 care-free years of smoking, drinking, junk food, tanning, and loud music finally catch up with you

- Health-emergency induced "life style changes"

- Going from worrying about looking hip to worrying about breaking your hip

- Bad genes that wait 50 years to announce their existence

- When every doctor visit buys your doctor another luxury car

"Old boys have their playthings as well as young ones; the difference is only in the price"

– Ben Franklin

- When the "sexual revolution" becomes a distant memory

- That your memory is the **second** thing to go

- When your spouse's sex drive shifts into low gear just as yours goes into high

- When sex and Friday the Thirteenth occur at about the same frequency

- Finally learning the truth of the saying, "Use it or lose it"

"Nature gives you the face you have at 20; it is up to you to merit the face you have at 50"

– Coco Chanel

- That the older you get, the smarter you were as a kid

- Carrying more gold in your mouth than on the rest of your body

- Getting beaten at computer games by a six-year-old

- Needing your teenager to load new computer programs for you

- Buying those "Dummy's Guide to Computers" books

That everything you learned in school has been obsolete for two decades

- Pop-psychology books for middle-agers by Gail Sheehy

- Knowing that Social Security will be belly-up by the time you retire

- Too many baby boomers vying for too few slots in upper management

- When the money you saved for a rainy day won't get you through a drizzle

"Life doesn't start at 40 or 50; it begins when you get one"

– Ed Strnad

- Seeing the TV shows you loved as a kid turned into moronic movies

- Remembering when the most popular family on the block was the one with the TV set

- Being bugged that soap operas don't use organ music anymore

- When you finally make the switch from "classic rock" radio stations to "easy listening"

- Getting the feeling that you have a great future behind you

TITLES BY CCC PUBLICATIONS

Blank Books ($3.99)
GUIDE TO SEX AFTER BABY
GUIDE TO SEX AFTER 30
GUIDE TO SEX AFTER 40
GUIDE TO SEX AFTER 50
GUIDE TO SEX AFTER MARRIAGE

Retail $4.95 – $4.99
"?" book
LAST DIET BOOK YOU'LL EVER NEED
CAN SEX IMPROVE YOUR GOLF?
THE COMPLETE BOOGER BOOK
FLYING FUNNIES
MARITAL BLISS & OXYMORONS
THE ADULT DOT-TO-DOT BOOK
THE DEFINITIVE FART BOOK
THE COMPLETE WIMP'S GUIDE TO SEX
THE CAT OWNER'S SHAPE UP MANUAL
THE OFFICE FROM HELL
FITNESS FANATICS
YOUNGER MEN ARE BETTER THAN RETIN-A
BUT OSSIFER, IT'S NOT MY FAULT
YOU KNOW YOU'RE AN OLD FART WHEN...
1001 WAYS TO PROCRASTINATE
HORMONES FROM HELL II
SHARING THE ROAD WITH IDIOTS
THE GREATEST ANSWERING MACHINE MESSAGES
WHAT DO WE DO NOW??
HOW TO TALK YOU WAY OUT OF A TRAFFIC TICKET
THE BOTTOM HALF
LIFE'S MOST EMBARRASSING MOMENTS
HOW TO ENTERTAIN PEOPLE YOU HATE
YOUR GUIDE TO CORPORATE SURVIVAL
NO HANG-UPS (Volumes I, II & III – $3.95 ea.)
TOTALLY OUTRAGEOUS BUMPER-SNICKERS ($2.95)

Retail $5.95
30 – DEAL WITH IT!
40 – DEAL WITH IT!
50 – DEAL WITH IT!
60 – DEAL WITH IT!
OVER THE HILL – DEAL WITH IT!
SLICK EXCUSES FOR STUPID SCREW-UPS
SINGLE WOMEN VS. MARRIED WOMEN
TAKE A WOMAN'S WORD FOR IT
SEXY CROSSWORD PUZZLES
SO, YOU'RE GETTING MARRIED
YOU KNOW HE'S A WOMANIZING SLIMEBALL WHEN...
GETTING OLD SUCKS
WHY GOD MAKES BALD GUYS
OH BABY!
PMS CRAZED: TOUCH ME AND I'LL KILL YOU!
WHY MEN ARE CLUELESS
THE BOOK OF WHITE TRASH
THE ART OF MOONING
GOLFAHOLICS
CRINKLED 'N' WRINKLED
SMART COMEBACKS FOR STUPID QUESTIONS
YIKES! IT'S ANOTHER BIRTHDAY

SEX IS A GAME
SEX AND YOUR STARS
SIGNS YOUR SEX LIFE IS DEAD
MALE BASHING: WOMEN'S FAVORITE PASTIME
THINGS YOU CAN DO WITH A USELESS MAN
MORE THINGS YOU CAN DO WITH A USELESS MAN
RETIREMENT: THE GET EVEN YEARS
LITTLE INSTRUCTION BOOK OF THE RICH & FAMOUS
WELCOME TO YOUR MIDLIFE CRISIS
GETTING EVEN WITH THE ANSWERING MACHINE
ARE YOU A SPORTS NUT?
MEN ARE PIGS / WOMEN ARE BITCHES
THE BETTER HALF
ARE WE DYSFUNCTIONAL YET?
TECHNOLOGY BYTES!
50 WAYS TO HUSTLE YOUR FRIENDS
HORMONES FROM HELL
HUSBANDS FROM HELL
KILLER BRAS & Other Hazards Of The 50's
IT'S BETTER TO BE OVER THE HILL THAN UNDER IT
HOW TO REALLY PARTY!!!
WORK SUCKS!
THE PEOPLE WATCHER'S FIELD GUIDE
THE ABSOLUTE LAST CHANCE DIET BOOK
THE UGLY TRUTH ABOUT MEN
NEVER A DULL CARD
THE LITTLE BOOK OF ROMANTIC LIES

Retail $6.95
EVERYTHING I KNOW I LEARNED FROM TRASH TALK TV
IN A PERFECT WORLD
I WISH I DIDN'T...
THE TOILET ZONE
SIGNS / TOO MUCH TIME W / CAT
LOVE & MARRIAGE & DIVORCE
CYBERGEEK IS CHIC
THE DIFFERENCE BETWEEN MEN AND WOMEN
GO TO HEALTH!
NOT TONIGHT, DEAR, I HAVE A COMPUTER!
THINGS YOU WILL NEVER HEAR THEM SAY
THE SENIOR CITIZENS'S SURVIVAL GUIDE
IT'S A MAD MAD MAD SPORTS WORLD
THE LITTLE BOOK OF CORPORATE LIES
RED HOT MONOGAMY
LOVE DAT CAT
HOW TO SURVIVE A JEWISH MOTHER

Retail $7.95
WHY MEN DON'T HAVE A CLUE
LADIES, START YOUR ENGINES!
ULI STEIN'S "ANIMAL LIFE"
ULI STEIN'S "I'VE GOT IT BUT IT'S JAMMED"
ULI STEIN'S "THAT SHOULD NEVER HAVE HAPPENED"

NO HANG-UPS – CASSETTES   Retail $5.98
Vol. I: GENERAL MESSAGES (M or F)
Vol. II: BUSINESS MESSAGES (M or F)
Vol. III: 'R' RATED MESSAGES (M or F)
Vol. V: CELEBRI-TEASE